Learning to Manage

The Art of Headless Chicken Management

Learning to Manage

The Art of **Headless Chicken Management**

Elly Brewer and Mark Edwards

Viva Books
New Delhi | Mumbai | Chennai | Kolkata
Bengaluru | Hyderabad | Kochi | Guwahati

Indian Edition 2011

VIVA BOOKS PRIVATE LIMITED

- 4737/23 Ansari Road, Daryaganj, New Delhi 110 002
  E-mail: vivadelhi@vivagroupindia.net, Tel. 42242200
- 76, Service Industries, Shirvane, Sector 1, Nerul, Navi Mumbai 400 706
  E-mail: vivamumbai@vivagroupindia.net, Tel. 27721273, 27721274
- Jamals Fazal Chambers, 26 Greams Road, Chennai 600 006
  E-mail: vivachennai@vivagroupindia.net, Tel. 28290304, 28294241
- B-103, Jindal Towers, 21/1A/3 Darga Road, Kolkata 700 017
  E-mail: vivakolkata@vivagroupindia.net, Tel. 22836381, 22816713
- 7, Sovereign Park Apartments, 56-58, K. R. Road, Basavanagudi, Bengaluru 560 004
  E-mail: vivabangalore@vivagroupindia.net, Tel. 26607409, 26607410
- 101-102 Mughal Marc Apartments, 3-4-637 to 641, Narayanguda, Hyderabad 500 029
  E-mail: vivahyderabad@vivagroupindia.net, Tel. 27564481, 27564482
- First Floor, Beevi Towers, SRM Road, Kaloor, Kochi 682 018, Kerala
  E-mail: vivakochi@vivagroupindia.net, Tel: 0484-2403055, 2403056
- 232, GNB Road, Beside UCO Bank, Silpukhuri, Guwahati 781 003
  E-mail: vivaguwahati@vivagroupindia.net, Tel: 0361-2666386

www.vivagroupindia.com

Published by arrangement with
Thorogood Publishers Limited
10-12 Rivington Street
London EC2A 3DU
UK

ISBN : 978-81-309-1703-0

Published by Vinod Vasishtha for Viva Books Private Limited, 4737/23, Ansari Road, Daryaganj, New Delhi-110 002. Printed and bound by Anand Sons, Delhi.

The authors

Elly Brewer is an award winning comedy writer, who works in both television and the theatre. In her formative years, Elly toiled in advertising and sales promotion, before leaving to run her own company, writing and producing theatrical events for the corporate sector. Elly has five 0-levels, a driving licence and RSA Stage III typing. She also has a preference for milk chocolate, never plain. This book draws on Elly's experiences working with various Headless Chicken Managers.

Mark Edwards divides his time between journalism and communications consultancy. Currently deputy business editor of *The European*, he has been a columnist for *The Guardian*, *The Daily Mail* and *Esquire*, and contributed regularly to *The Sunday Times*, *The Face* and *Arena*. As a consultant, he advises companies within the communications industry on their own internal and external communications.

Contents

This book is a monument to the KEF* effect

A monument it may be – but is it for *you*? Since we've only just met you, we don't know enough about you to judge – although you seem pleasant enough. (Flattery is often a good motivator.)

Look, don't make any hasty decisions . . . work through the flow chart on the next page – that should tell you whether this book will be of interest to you or not.

* Knocking off Early on Fridays . . .

The First Flow Chart

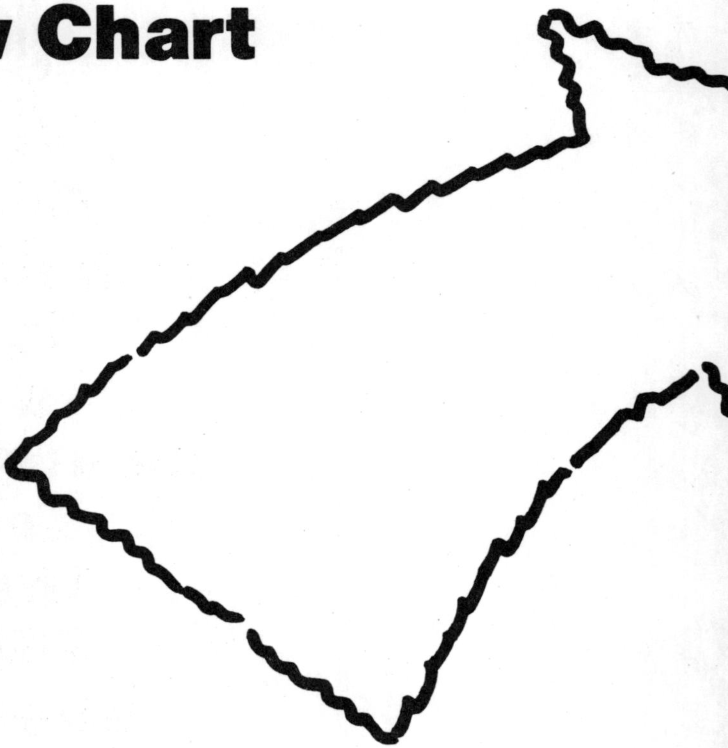

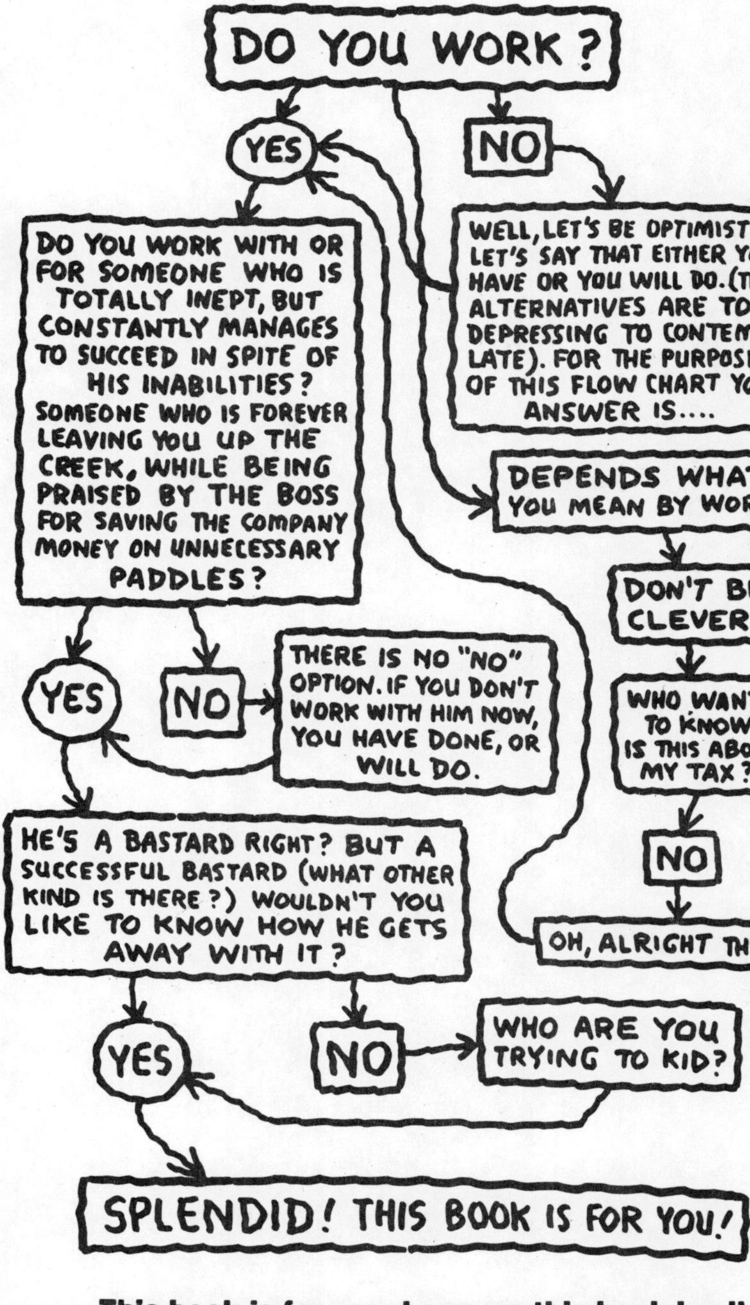

This book is for you, because this book is all about . . . (feel that tension building?) . . .

The Art of Headless Chicken Management

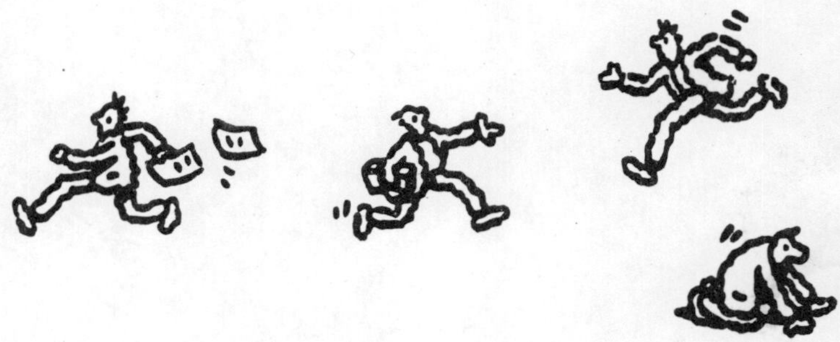

6

The Art of What . . .?

Good – you really do need this book. A Headless Chicken Manager would never admit that he didn't understand something that had just been said.

He would smile, nod wisely and say, 'Ah, I see the old HCM technique is back on the scene again' – rather than concede that he'd never heard of the concept.

Other working practices that typify a Headless Chicken Manager include:

- refusing to read the document that's taken you three weeks to prepare, then asking you for a summary, five minutes before the meeting, so that he can present the information . . . as his own;
- making three-point plans with four points, two of which are totally irrelevant and one of which, if implemented, would cause civil war in South America;
- claiming responsibility for your successes and blaming others for all his failures;
- double booking meetings in different parts of town, or even different continents. (And turning up to neither.)

Starting to recognise him?

He's the one man in your office who spends 110% of his life acting like a Headless Chicken (at last – the point) to compensate for his inefficiency and total incompetence. And with the inevitable ripple effect that such behaviour triggers, forces everyone else to shoulder the burden created by his directionless activities.

But the Headless Chicken Manager's conduct goes beyond mere compensation for ineptitude. More importantly, it covers it up – because the one characteristic, above all others, by which you can identify an HCM is that **He Always Gets Away With It**.

If you *do* recognise this man, the one question you'll have asked yourself over and over again is:

HOW DOES HE ALWAYS GET AWAY WITH IT?

It has been said that the best way to learn is through example, so we're going to show you how to identify a classic HCM in your own company, by pointing out the techniques to watch for, so that you can look, listen and learn, and ultimately develop your own personalised Headless Chicken Management style.

This should give you the confidence to throw away all those incomprehensible management books, yet still enable you to rise above the common herd. (And this is not a time for levity.)

One small matter – you must be absolutely certain that your chosen HCM is an honours graduate in this subject and not simply a new boy – after all, you're not the only one who may have just discovered this book.

Fortunately for you, old habits die hard (and old

cliches die hardest) so you'll be able to spot trainee HCMs by their brief displays of rather Jekyll and Hydeish behaviour, as they veer between professionalism and incompetence in their quest to arrive at the HCM level which suits them best.

In contrast, the true HCM is *always* totally useless and totally ruthless, with no brief displays of anything.

There you have it then, it's as easy as 'a, b, three' – just find yourself a genuine HCM, emulate like fury and your future career advancement is guaranteed.

Oh and by the way – don't strike out on your own until you're absolutely sure of yourself. We cannot be held responsible for those disciples who out-chicken themselves onto the end of the dole queue.

We are, as any HCM would tell you, 'merely floating some sail boats on the duck pond, to see if any make it to the other shore'. Picking up said sail boat and running away with it, was entirely your own idea. And brave though that was – and much as we admire you for that bravery – oh, you know . . . make up the rest yourselves . . .

Lesson one: delegation

Footnote:

You may have thought you noticed a sexist tone to our scenario (buzz word*). Well, you're right.

Our exhaustive research has shown that the majority of Headless Chicken Managers are men. There *are* successful, yet incompetent, women around but they employ different techniques to appear impressive. (There may be another book there – and if this one sells, there will be.)

Given the male bias of *this* book, perhaps we should have called it 'The Art of Headless Cock Management', but the Freudian implications were too dreadful to contemplate.

* There'll be another buzz word along in a minute.

The Second Flow Chart

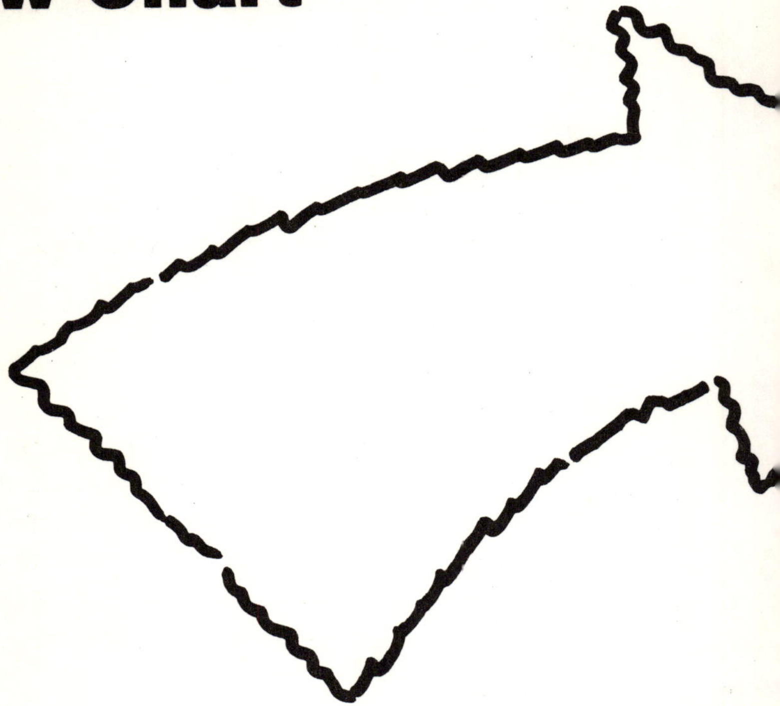

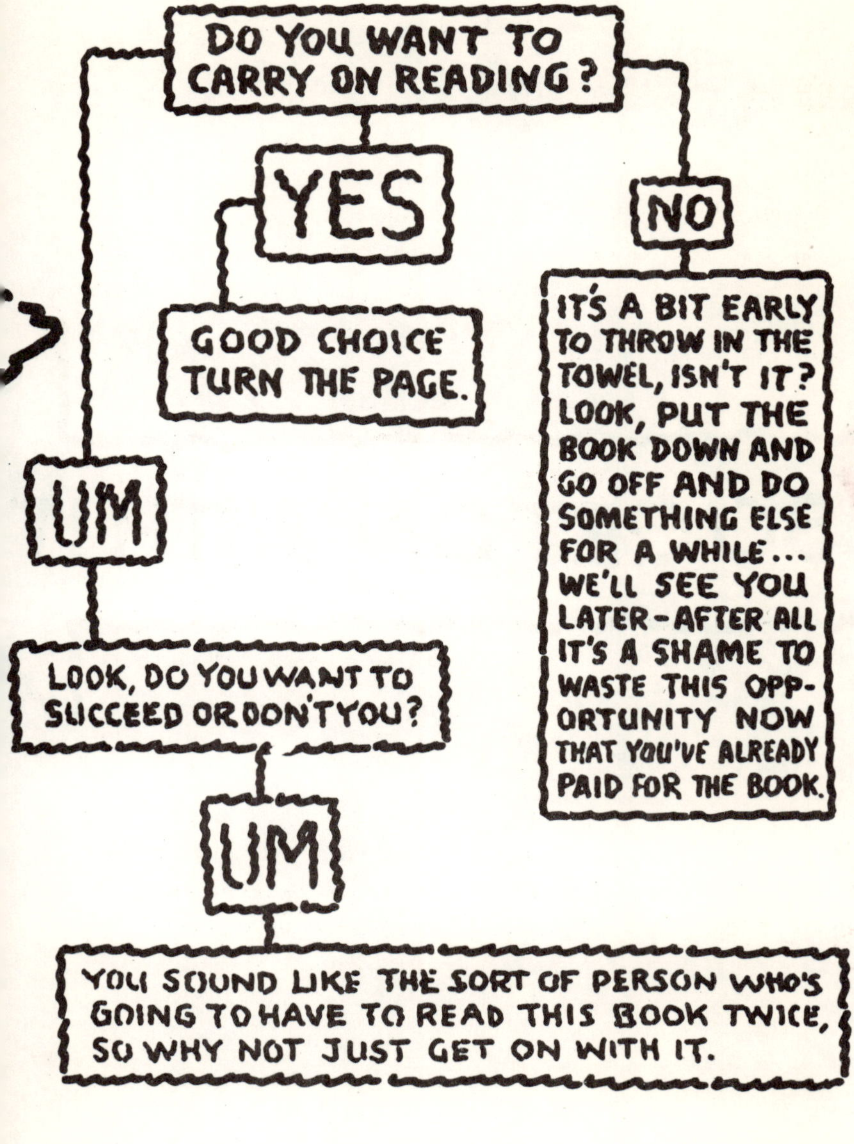
DO YOU WANT TO CARRY ON READING?
YES
NO
UM
GOOD CHOICE TURN THE PAGE.
IT'S A BIT EARLY TO THROW IN THE TOWEL, ISN'T IT? LOOK, PUT THE BOOK DOWN AND GO OFF AND DO SOMETHING ELSE FOR A WHILE... WE'LL SEE YOU LATER - AFTER ALL IT'S A SHAME TO WASTE THIS OPPORTUNITY NOW THAT YOU'VE ALREADY PAID FOR THE BOOK.
LOOK, DO YOU WANT TO SUCCEED OR DON'T YOU?
UM
YOU SOUND LIKE THE SORT OF PERSON WHO'S GOING TO HAVE TO READ THIS BOOK TWICE, SO WHY NOT JUST GET ON WITH IT.

SO GET ON WITH IT

Scene the First. In which we meet Joe Manager, a star graduate of the Headless Chicken School of Management. But nobody else does.

'I'm *so* sorry, but the line's *still* busy *and* there's another call holding. Would you mind calling back later? Er, yes, if you like . . . I'll just try again for you.'

Suzy, Joe Manager's ever-efficient, hard-working, child-minder – her job description says 'secretary', but then it also says she gets a lunch hour – buzzes through to Joe's office.

'Joe? Mr Brownlow is insisting that he talks to you – couldn't you just have a quick word?'

'There's no such thing as a quick word, in my book, Suzy – I told you, I'm not to be disturbed.'

CLICK.

'Mr Brownlow? I'm *really* sorry, but Mr Manager is still on the other line and I can see from here that it's going to be a long one. Could I take a message and get him to call you?'

(Yes – and no. She could take a message, but he'll never return the call.)

'Yes, well, you see, he really was *ever* so busy yesterday – we had a bit of a crisis on, you know how it can be sometimes, but I have made him fully aware that you're trying to speak to him. Yes, yes, I will. Thank you so much, Mr Brownlow, goodbye.'

Suzy replaces the Trim-phone Mellow-tone handset on the XR47 Dominator Executive Switchboard[1] and smiles sympathetically at two rather bored executives who are sitting opposite her in Joe's outer office.

'I'm sure he won't keep you much longer – you just wouldn't believe how snowed under he's been this morning.'

The more important looking (but still bored) executive–the one in the double breasted suit – shifts irritably in his seat. 'Look, could you remind him again that we're here?' Double Breasted pouts petulantly. 'After all, it was *him* that asked *us* to come to this meeting.'

'At very short notice' – chimes in his colleague, angrily scratching some mud off the trouser leg of his cheap shiny suit.

'I mean, we don't even know why we're here', blusters Double Breasted. 'If we knew what he wanted, we could have been thinking about it while we've been parked on our bums here for the last thirty minutes.'

'Thirty-five,' corrects Shiny Suit piously.

Suzy buzzes through to Joe again.

Footnote: (See page 19)

'Joe? Shall I make you a black without, while I'm making coffee for Mark and Tony ... *who are out here waiting to see you?*'

'Waiting to see me? Waiting to see me? What the devil are they waiting to see me for?'

'Er, just taking you off Conference, Joe. Didn't you ask them to pop in ...'

'Drop everything and get over here NOW' – Double Breasted mutters to himself from his end of the pock marked leatherette-look two seater.

'... because you weren't entirely happy with the way the figures were stacking up in the latest research audit?'

'Research? Don't bother me with research now, Suzy. You're just going to have to make my apologies and re-fix – I think there's a breakfast window in my Filo for Thursday. Thanks duckie – and get me a black without, would you? Honestly, a bloke could die of thirst in this place ...'

'Yes, Joe.'

Suzy replaces the phone, somewhat sharply, and turns to Double Breasted and Shiny Suit. She's just about to enter Standard Apology Mode (Recipient Rage Level 3)[2] as a loud tie, closely followed by a frantic man, bursts into the room, clutching a sheaf of papers.

Footnote: (See page 19)

'Scuse me, fellas. Suzy – Joe got anyone with him? I've negotiated that discount he wanted and if I don't get his signature on these orders now, I can't give Manchester the green light and we'll lose the special rate.' Loud Tie snaps the sheaf of papers enthusiastically with the back of his free hand.

'Sorry, John, but he's rather tied up at the moment. I don't think he's going to thank me for disturbing him again.'

'He's not going to thank you if he has to pay an extra $12\frac{1}{2}$% on this order, either,' barks Loud Tie, waving the papers so close to Suzy's chin that the corner of a page catches in a rather deep dimple. 'Just buzz him for me, would you, love?'

Suzy reluctantly lifts up the phone.

'Joe? Er, I've got John the Accountant out here, he wondered if . . .

'I don't care if you've got John the bloody Baptist out there – I told you not to disturb me under any circumstances.' Joe's disembodied voice spirals from a whine to a roar and reverberates around the tiny outer office. **'Why doesn't anybody ever listen to a word I say?'**[3]

Slam . . . dialling tone.

Footnote: (See page 19)

'Er, I think you're going to have to leave those papers with me, John. Joe seems to be right in the middle of something.' Suzy smiles a little too brightly.

'I only want a lousy signature, that's not exactly going to take him very long, is it – even if he makes a special effort and does joined up writing.'

Loud Tie sweeps past Suzy and tries to breeze through Joe's office door, nearly flattening his nose in the process. He grunts in surprise at finding the door firmly locked, but recovers enough to take a well aimed kick with a tired old Hush Puppie, which yelps in protest at the impact. The door doesn't even provide the satisfaction of a scuff mark.

Loud Tie pivots, cheeks pink with rage and hurls the papers onto Suzy's desk. He stalks out, talking over a dandruffed shoulder as he goes. 'It's taken me two days solid to get that soddin' price down. You can tell him from me – I've done all I can. The ball's in his court and

I refuse to carry the bloody can when the chickens come home to soddin' well roost.'[4] He slams the outer office door with the strength of the self-righteous and stalks off down the corridor.

Suzy pats a temporary perm and gives a nervous laugh. 'And they say women are emotional!'

Let's go through the tinted window and see what it is that has gripped Our Hero in such a fever of activity this morning . . .

The sunlight streams through the picture window behind Joe's desk. Not a sound can be heard, save the gentle rustle of a turning page and the high-pitched squeak of highlighter pen on paper.

Joe leans back in his chair with his feet, casually crossed at the ankles, resting on the edge of his desk, reading a book: *Leading the Team – A Guide for Today's Manager.*

Squeak, squeak, squeak – Joe methodically wields a thick yellow highlighting pen over the last paragraph of Chapter Four – 'The Open Door'.

> *Communication is everything in today's business world – and today's successful manager should be accessible to all of his staff, all of the time.*

Nodding to himself, Joe makes a thick yellow tick under the paragraph, then re-caps his highlighter and closes the book. Standing to replace it in his bookcase, he smiles, then carefully creates a space between *Working Together – The Boss as Buddy* and *Hands On Management – The Velvet Glove Approach.*

'Somebody's obviously been watching Old Joe at work,' he thinks to himself smugly.

Ah yes, another productive morning . . .

Footnotes:

[1] As ordered specifically by Joe. See Executive Toys. (It's something akin to impotency, pulling away fast at traffic lights, and The Phallic Symbol as Management Tool.)

[2] The HCM's secretary has a set of standard apologies, depending on who her boss has offended and how deeply he has offended them. These two factors are measured in terms of Recipient Rage Levels 1–9. (How angry are they? Can their anger be used against her Boss?)

For example, a furious post boy requires less apology than a mildly irritated Managing Director—unless said post boy is the aforementioned Managing Director's son, or he's carrying a loaded firearm. (If confronted by a gun-toting post boy, who also happens to be the Managing Director's son, stall like crazy until 'The HCM's Guide to Rage Deflection' reaches the shops.)

[3] Paranoia. (And quite right too.)

[4] Mixed metaphor denotes Genuine Fear. He knows the chicken's going to roost on his shoulder and nobody's going to believe they weren't his bird droppings.

Executive Summary

So, what have we learnt from all this? (apart from how to write patronising headlines)

1

That 'Old Joe' thinks he's the most approachable bloke on the block.

2

That he's got virtually no memory.

3

That he drinks black without.

4

That we shouldn't patronise the reader.

OK, we won't. To understand a little more about the HCM, we need to study his office, or lair. (A bit like one of those nature programmes, where they stick cameras in unbelievable places and spy on wildlife performing any number of unsavoury acts.)

De-coding the desk

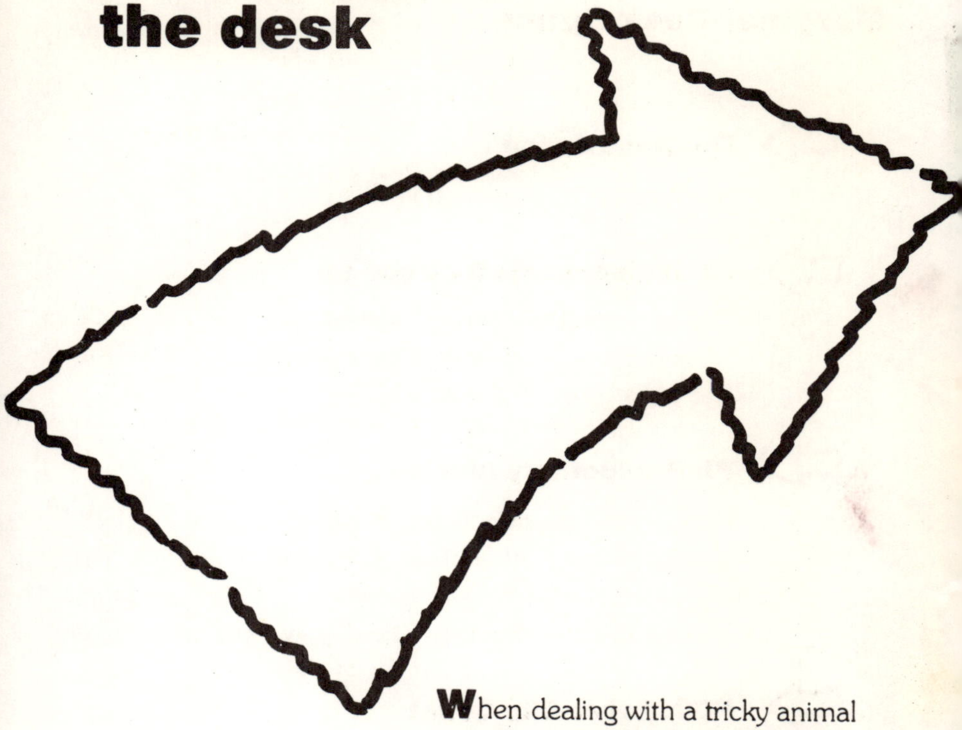

When dealing with a tricky animal like the HCM, it helps to get an idea of what is going on inside his head. A useful guide to this is the state of the HCM's surroundings (see now how the nature allegory works) – mostly notably, his desk.

The Law of Diminishing Marginal Desk Space

Key:

DS: Desk Space

Amount of space available.

IQ: Indispensability Quotient

This is a measure of how, as his desk becomes more cluttered, the HCM feels more needed. Note that this line goes through the roof.

PI: Productivity Illusion

PI is a measure of how much work the HCM *thinks* he is doing. Note that as PI rises, E (efficiency) falls. Yes, we know 'efficiency' is a misnomer, it's purely a relative measurement, since the HCM is never actually efficient.

PCC: Paper Clip Count

See how the PCC rises on Fridays when the HCM makes paper clip daisy chains during the weekly Departmental Overview meetings. Because the HCM deals in 'Broad Strategy' only. (See the IPTDIBSO Effect on page 59.)

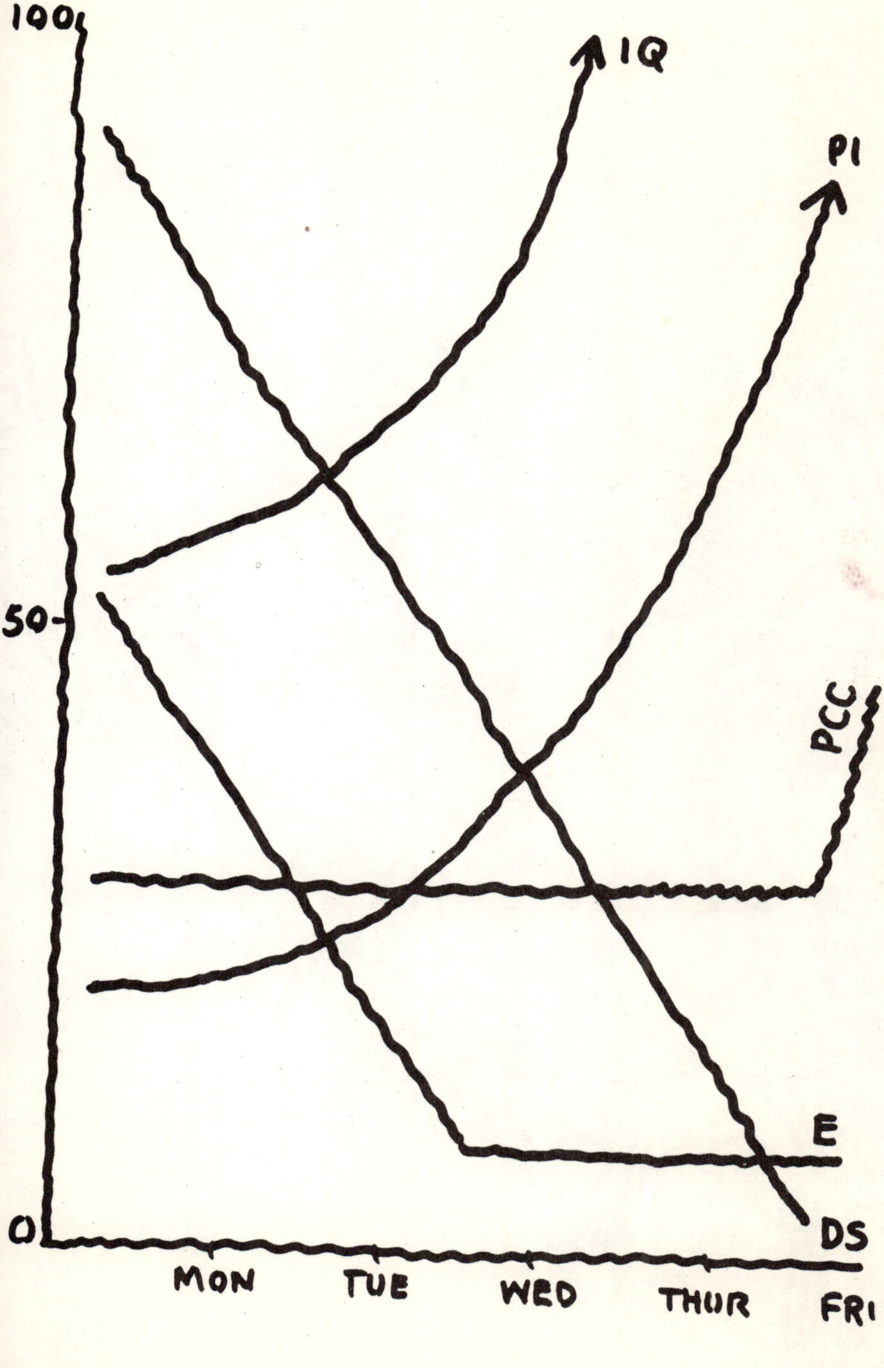
100
50
0
IQ
PI
PCC
E
DS
MON
TUE
WED
THUR
FRI

23

You're probably wondering how Joe's desk is clear again by Monday (he never wonders – he still believes in the Clutter Fairy). Suzy (for it is she) comes in early every Monday morning to tidy the desk and return documents and papers to their rightful owners, all of which Joe has emphatically denied having throughout the previous week.

The HCM as Lost Property Office

A small, but useful point to remember: HCMs attract other people's paperwork, possessions, packets of biscuits and tea money like a sink attracts stubble. If he denies having it – he's got it, because he's got everything, possessionwise.

Denial as a means of honesty evasion

Not so much a lie, more a way of life

We're not necessarily saying you should cultivate a messy desk habit (unless you have one already) – although confusion is often a useful camouflage and can be cited as evidence for your claim to be 'creative'. What we're really saying is, don't worry about losing anything. Just deny you ever had it in the first place – after all, lost property is bound to turn up sooner or later (look what happened with the Mary Rose) and let's face it, if the work's that important, someone will always do it again.

So that's covered the HCM's desk – or has it? Before the suspense gives you indigestion, we'll tell you that it hasn't.

There's one powerful, vicious weapon, that sits throbbing and menacing on the corner of the desk, which if put in the wrong hands, can destroy a man's career faster than a married politician's jilted girlfriend.

Yes, you've guessed it – Alexander Graham Telephone's invention.

The Telephone

The Headless Chicken Manager is a Master in the Art of Telecommunication. That's if you can get past his secretary. Because all his calls are normally incoming, since the HCM rarely makes calls himself, or returns other people's – not until the third or fourth time you've rung, anyway. (Unless the caller is further up the pecking order, that is.)

And the reason why he doesn't make calls is that making telephone calls is a sign of weakness. If you phone someone, it's because you want something. And asking someone for something puts you at an immediate disadvantage.

Remember, it's only the recipient of a call who can legitimately use the 'I'll have to put you on hold for a second' or 'I'm on the other line, I'll have to get back to you' weapons, with their implied message 'you can't be as important as me, because I have to deal with something else before I talk to you.

However, there are those rare moments when the HCM has sent his secretary off on one of those important little errands, like collecting his dry cleaning, or buying his mother's birthday present, when people do get through direct. And you have to admire the way a skilled HCM handles such situations. We call it 'Power Chatting' and it's a very valuable technique in the Art of Headless Chicken Management.

Power Chatting

'I'm busy. Joe Manager. What d'you want? Oh hallo! How odd that you've phoned me – you're right at the top of my list of calls for today. No, no, that's all right . . . just in a meet with some people, but they can wait – can't you lads? Sure, sure, nothing important anyway.

How's your love life? What? Oh that. Er, no, no, I haven't had time to look at it. Yes, I do realize how important it is, but Suzy had me in meets all last week, and frankly this week's not looking so rosy either, but honestly, I promise I'll get round to it asap.

Eh? Oh! Er, sure thing, no problem – yeah, have mine talk to yours. Oh look, I'd better go – I'm supposed to be in this meet and the lads are getting restless. Oh, nothing, no big deal, everybody wants to talk to Old Joe – Sure, I'll buzz you back . . . ten minutes, tops. See you later, mate, ciao.'

It's amazing how many HCM techniques can be crammed into such a short phone call.

Firstly

See how the first four words establish who's in charge and intimidate straight away. It lets the humble caller know that they've interrupted somebody who's Very Busy. Even if you're totally unimportant, answering the phone with 'I'm busy' forces the caller to act as if you are – and makes him doubt the worth of his call.

Secondly

The use of **'you're at the top of my list of calls for today'**. Obviously it's a complete lie – but who's going to challenge it? And it makes the caller feel that Joe had been thinking about him, which is a crucial HCM technique because it staves off recriminations, since Joe was clearly 'just about to' do whatever it was he was supposed to have done weeks ago.

Thirdly

The use of the line **'Suzy had me in meets all last week'**. This is the office equivalent of inverted snobbery. Who instigated all those meetings, anyway? But it still makes it sound like there were a lot of people out there who wanted to seek old Joe's advice about various matters.

The fourth

HCM technique is the use of the dreaded 'ASAP' to avoid any commitment to the caller. At the end of the conversation, we have no clearer idea when Joe will look at the document.

Admire too the deflectionary tactic of **'have mine talk to yours'**. The caller is still trying to pin Joe down about some work he should have done, by fixing a meeting. Joe tells him to have his secretary talk to Joe's secretary. He implies that the matter is in hand, but that it's simply too trivial for two such important businessmen to discuss– let the women handle it.

Finally

One of the HCM's favourites – the throwaway insult: **'I'd better go – I'm supposed to be in this meet and the lads are getting restless ... oh nothing, no big deal ... ten minutes, tops'**.

Once he's realized that the caller is a friend, he no longer feels the need to intimidate him (at least on this occasion). But HCMs are so insecure, they're incapable of going for five minutes without establishing their superiority to somebody (in the absence of any living beings, office furniture will suffice – what do you imagine executive toys are all about?).

Therefore, there is a scattering of comments to make it clear to the people in his office that the HCM really doesn't think they merit spending much time on, and that the meeting which should be receiving his complete attention is the least important item on his mind.

As well as all these individual points, let's look at the overall balance of the conversation. Count how many words Joe spoke (or get somebody else to count them for you). Now extrapolate the number of words you think the person on the other end of the line might have squeezed in (or – carry on the good work – appoint three subordinates, all of whom have far more important things to do, to form a working party to look into the possible number of imaginary words and report back to you). Clearly, Joe overwhelmed his opponent in that vital **Words Per Call (WPC)** factor.

If you talk loud enough and fast enough, the caller will spend most of the call trying to get a word in edgewise, which will thoroughly distract him from what it was he'd phoned about in the first place.

Mobile phones

Here the HCM finds himself torn between his love affair with new technology (irrespective of an ability to make it function) and the chaos that always ensues when he plays with a ringing phone.

Luckily there is a perfect accessory for the busy Headless Chicken Manager with a mobile phone that he cannot bear to answer: **the mobile answerphone**.

It means that when all those thrusting executives meet for lunch and place their mobile phones in the centre of the table, the HCM simply attaches his to a battery operated mobile answerphone.

That way he can hear who the caller is, without having to answer the call personally. And there's the added snob value of pretending he's on the other line, when the caller knows for certain that he's dialled a mobile phone.

The crucial point for would-be HCMs to remember about the telephone is – when the bell rings, come out fighting.

Anyway, telephones are for secretaries – unless you're trying to ask a woman out, and that would take a whole chapter of its own. And don't confuse secretaries with women – that would be a very dangerous mistake, because that road leads to Matrimoney.

My Secretary and Other Animals

Secretaries – funny creatures. They don't really fall into any other category but their own. And they're vital to the HCM. Not that he'd ever admit it. Not that he'd ever realize it.

Most of you probably appreciate the support that a really good secretary can provide. Well, for an HCM, this support is not so much a walking stick, it's more of an iron lung.

A well-trained HCM's secretary is . . .

NURSE, AGONY AUNT, MOTHER, COFFEE MAKER, SQUASH COURT BOOKER AND DEFENDER OF ALL THAT THE HCM SURVEYS.

But as far as an HCM is concerned, she's just there. Doing the job she's over-paid for.

Which is useful really, because hers is the open door at which any amount of blame may be heaped. And that's one of her key functions, because HCMs are always – now how can we put this delicately . . . economical with the truth. We're talking negative accuracy here.

The truth as pop music

BEND IT, SHAPE IT, ANYWAY YOU WANT IT

HCMs are great believers in 'bending the truth'. And that's not just the little white lies that most people employ at work. These are the thumping great whoppers whose sheer audacity leaves you gasping and listening for the thunderclap.

Because the dyed-in-the-wool HCM is probably one of the few people you'll come across in business, who will confidently tell you white is black and when challenged look wounded and deny with a cherubic look of innocence, that he ever said any such thing. Or remind you that, anyway, it all depends on your definition of 'black' and 'white'.

And it's this 'black is white' principle – or 'BWP' – that applies to his secretary. Missed deadlines, unfinished documents, hours late for meetings, double booked lunches. You name it – his secretary forgot to do it.

The perfect set-up. Why? Because how could she

remember – the HCM never asked her in the first place. And should she ever find out that he's blamed her, she knows from previous experience that there's no point confronting her boss, because he'll deny it (remember the BWP?). Like we said – perfect!

The secretary is the next stage on for those situations where a **Standard Denial Tactic** simply won't wash. If you need a slightly more sophisticated approach (or you've denied something once too often) experiment with good old-fashioned Blame. Add a dash of Righteous Indignation, with a pinch of Sincerity and you'll have really cooked her goose.

Now budding HCMs mustn't be squeamish about testing these theories, since there is actually a profitable purpose in cultivating such a callous attitude towards your secretary. You're only being cruel to be kind, to toughen her up and help her cultivate her skills, self-preservationwise.

Then she'll watch you, your diary and your workload like a hawk to make sure that everything runs like clockwork, simply as a preventative measure against you getting into a mess and blaming it on her. Brilliant – the Secretary as Scapegoat Principle, or 'SSP'.*

As we illustrated earlier, the SSP also comes into operation when the secretary deals with the HCM's outer office. And this doesn't have to be a literal outer office – the concept is more global than that – it's . . .

the Headless Chicken Manager
versus
the Rest of the World.

*** Don't worry about remembering all our Buzz Initials – we'll do a Filofax Memory Jogger, or FMJ, at the end.**

I'm OK– Who Cares About You?

Like any self respecting Headless Chicken Manager, your philosophy in life should mirror this statement. We say 'life' rather than 'work', because in our experience the true HCM makes no distinctions between the two. It's not that he's so dedicated that he's a workaholic – far from it. It's more that his HCMness is a personality trait which is so much a part of his character, that it would be easier to stop him breathing, than behaving in this way.

Cowardy Custard trainee HCMs who intend to maintain a modicum of 'niceness' outside their work, can always cut their philosophy cloth to suit. (And if you choose Petticoat Lane as opposed to Savile Row, who are we to cast the first herringbone?)

But one rule is sacrosanct – you must evolve a range of attitudes, each to be adopted according to the seniority of the person or people present. After all, you'd be foolish to treat your boss with the same cursory manner tossed away on the company security man.

We know how important these attitudes are, from observing the HCM inter-relating (buzz word) with other people and noting how, roughly speaking, he subconsciously divides them into three categories:

1 **Superiors and clients**

2 **Colleagues or subordinates (no real distinction between the two)**

3 **Outside suppliers**

4 **Secretaries and animals**

Superiors and clients

Well, there's only so much toadying a person can do – or is there? The HCM seems to find new ways with every passing day.

A skilled HCM knows how to pull out all the stops when dealing with people who are higher up the corporate ladder, or who pay him money for work (other people's, that is). If anyone's going to walk under that ladder, it won't be him.

Unlike dealing with his inferiors (as he likes to call them), where it's as much as he can do to even remember what sex they are, let alone any morsel of personal information – when it comes to making small talk with superiors or fee-paying clients, no detail is too microscopically trivial for consideration.

“How is Mrs Potter's Egyptian Orchid? Did the gardener manage to save it? I'm so glad. And did the decorator manage to squeeze an extra wall from that tin of Easy Iris? Thank goodness – such a calming shade, I've always thought.”

The more you remember – the more you show you care. Or to put it another way . . . people remember people who remember. Right? Right. And they don't realise that in answering your banal enquiry, they've been diverted from the main tack, which is probably why you haven't done something on time/budget/fill in as appropriate.

A Quiz

Yes, here's one of those irritating little quizzes – and why not, they take up lots of space and we haven't had one yet – to test your triviality rating.

See how you rate – if you score **100 or higher**, you know more about your boss and/or client than his/her mother. Play it carefully though, you don't want to be named in a paternity suit.

Forty-five or less and you're really missing a trick. Bone up on the old trout and flash a few 'I'm a warm, caring, individual so I must be good at my job' type enquiries around the room.

As well as points, you can also acquire Ferrari Tokens. These are self-explanatory, so let's explain them: the more 'FTs' you collect, the better the company car you'll be driving in three years time. Twelve FTs or more and it'll be a Ferrari. No FTs ... no phallus extension.

The quiz is all purpose, but has been set out here to apply to bosses, because most people have one. However, if you're self employed, pretend the questions apply to your bank manager or accountant – that should do the trick.

If you're really stuck, use your wife or partner for test purposes. People with bosses *and* clients (how some people suffer) may use the same questions for both parties (although do avoid this gambit if you're with the two together – they may smell rancid poultry).

Note particularly how Toadying and Blackmail are different sides of the same can of boot polish. At its best (most productive, careerwise), Toadying isn't being nice – it's *not* being nasty. But conspicuously.

Here we go then, pencils ready? No? We'll just insert another small section then, while you go off to find one.

In praise of pencil

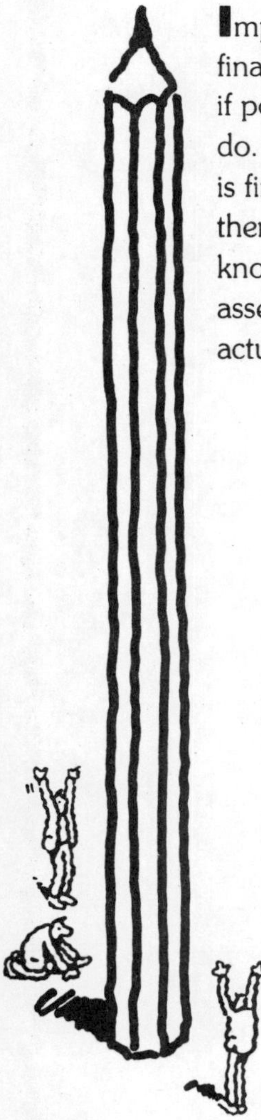

Important point: never do anything in pen – it's so terribly final and always smudges when you try to rub it out. Also, if possible, never sign your name yourself. HCMs never do. Get someone else to 'pp' your signature – a secretary is fine for this task and usually most obliging (it makes them feel important). At least then you can deny all knowledge afterwards. It's always so difficult to try and assert that something that is exactly like your signature is actually a forgery.

Trivia For Suits

Boss's name:

Surname ____________________ Score: 5 points

First name ____________________ 10 points

Nickname at school ____________________ 15 points

Nickname at school (but swear never to tell anyone else in the company)

____________________ 20 points/2 FTs

Partner's name:

(ex husbands/wives/lovers don't count, since you should never be the first to bring them up in conversation)

First name ____________________ 5 points

Surname ____________________ 10 points
(more difficult, in these liberated times)

Name they prefer to be called at moments of extreme sexual stimulation

____________________ 25 points/5 FTs*

* Assuming, that is, that you never, ever, utter the name in your boss's presence. The high score reflects the endless scope for Career Improving Blackmail, or 'CIB', that your obvious degree of intimacy with his/her partner gives you. Beware however, the Jilted Lover Syndrome – if you want to end the affair before they're ready – you're business history.

Offspring:

Boys 2 points age ____________________ 4 points

name ______________________________ 4 points

Girls 2 points age ____________________ 4 points

name ______________________________ 4 points

Although it's better to know the actual name, gender will suffice, as in 'how's your lovely daughter/clever son'.

Name of school/university attended

______________________________ 6 points

Name of therapist/social worker/probation officer, where appropriate

______________________________ 10 points/2 FTs

Pets:

Type: ______________________________ 3 points

Name: ______________________________ 10 points

Always remember who the pet belongs to. If it's your boss's then enquire with concerned interest. If it's your boss's partner's, the chances are your boss hates it – assume an air of comradely jocularity, as in 'are you still putting Fifi's dinner on the other side of the road?'

Hobbies:

Type: ______________________________ 3 points

No high score for remembering this – people with hobbies usually bleat on about them incessantly. Merely put here as a reminder of a potential topic. However, only to be mentioned if the hobby is suitable for a family audience. (Do remember other types though, they're useful CIBs if you find yourself in a sticky corner.)

Milestones:

First job ______________________________ 5 points

First major career breakthrough______________________

______________________________ 10 points*

First sexual encounter________________ 15 points/5 FTs

* As in: 'you know, Derek, if you pull this off, it'll be another Hounslow for you'; or, 'first Birmingham Sales and now Manchester Resources – not many of us get two bites at the cherry, old chap'.

By now you should be getting an idea of the type of Topic for Toadying, or 'TT', that we have in mind. And the Obviously Useful Career Helpers, or 'OUCH' topics, that should be avoided (as long as your boss knows you're avoiding them). We're sure you can make up a few of your own, even though it goes against the grain for an HCM to ever do anything on his own. But as you're starting out, perhaps we'll make an exception.

If the list had continued, it would have included topics like:

make and colour of car/partner's car

interior decoration of office/house

musical tastes

ethnic food preferences (anything that isn't British)

holiday destinations

recent operations (last five years)

and so on ...

Gosh, you're really going to make a super HCM, you've just persuaded us to give you more ideas than we'd meant to! (In an inspirational vacuum, flattery provides a reliable airpocket.)

Use the quiz as a guide (but don't take it into meetings with you) and on the pure Toadying side, memorise the following points for your mental check-list:

- always keep it personal (as in 'how are *you*?' not 'you haven't asked me how *I* am');
- the more trivial the enquiry, the higher the metaphorical score;
- try not to be offensive with your intrusions.

Colleagues and inferiors

Let's look at colleagues first.

If we were writing this book from the other point of view, we could write reams covering what his colleagues think about the HCM. How thoughtless, stupid, sneaky, tiresome ... voice a derogatory adjective and there's always an HCM to shout it at. But that's not what we're here for, so put down that Thesaurus.

If you're to succeed as a Headless Chicken Manager, you have to forget all about your colleagues – ignore everything they ask you to do and carry on as if you're the only person in the company.

You can't get much more succinct than that, now can you?

Yes, probably – never be precise about anything, you'll almost definitely want to change your mind afterwards. So, let's rephrase it and this time let's ...

QUALIFY,

QUALIFY,

QUALIFY.

'As at this moment in time, we are certainly unaware of any legitimately applicable prior instances of such succincticity, within the broad parameters within which we have been working, up until now.'

As for inferiors

Well, they're there to serve. Aren't they? So pretty much the same manner should be applied as for colleagues, except you can boss this lot around, whereas you can only attempt to boss your colleagues around.

Of course, you could try and persuade people to like you by being a bit more considerate, but then you wouldn't be a true HCM.

Outside suppliers

Bit of a tricky one, this. There's no point ignoring them, because they're another source of work placement, so that you don't have to do it yourself. But you pay them (or you're supposed to) – and since payment demands servility from the payee, there's no need to toady.

So, how best to deal with this peculiar classification? Well, the typical HCM keeps the meetings brief and the briefs miniscule so that if – oh, optimistic writers – *when* things go wrong, the HCM can beat his breast with equanimity and proclaim that they misinterpreted the brief – AGAIN!

Perhaps the best way of showing you how to deal with outside suppliers is to introduce dear Joe back into the frame (buzz phrase) and let him show you how it's done. . . .

Friday: 10.00 am
Meeting with Markup and Hustle

In which Joe meets up with his sales promotion agency and tells them about A Very Good Idea. And they 'take it on board' – whether they've docked yet or not . . .

Motes of dust rise from the carpet as Frank Markup's leather (genuine Italian) loafers pad up and down reception. A discreet beeping emits from Dave Hustle's wrist. Pushing back his gold bracelets, Dave turns off the

alarm on his thirty-seven-function IBM compatible digital wrist-management system and sighs.

The receptionist looks up from coating her nails with a second layer of Passion Flower Purple. 'More coffee?'

'No thanks, love. Look, he does know we're here, doesn't he?' (*Sound familiar?*)

'Oh yes, Mr Hustle. I buzzed through when you arrived . . .'

'. . . that *was* an hour ago.'

'I know, but he's been brainstorming (buzz concept) with the Chief Exec since early this morning and I . . .'

The revolving doors revolve, propelling a dishevelled Joe Manager into reception.

'Carol – hi! D'you know, I've just spent half an hour driving up and down, trying to get a bloody meter. I tell you – oh, hallo lads. Nice to see you got here early . . . for once.'

(*Notice here the use of the 'compound insult'. Before the meeting has even begun, Joe has managed to offend his agency twice, in the same sentence. First of all – he's late. We know it, they know it and he knows it. But from his opening remark, we all realize he's never going to admit it. Secondly, Joe has implied, with just two words, that the agency are always late.*)

'Come on up. Need any help? Good.' Joe strides off towards the lift, while Dave and Frank scrabble for their briefcases and artbags.

'Actually, Joe,' says Frank, juggling luggage, 'the meeting was booked for . . .'

'Lift's here – come on fellas, don't lag behind.'

'… 10.00' finishes Dave, wincing miserably as the pointy end of a heavy briefcase finds the most tender part of his big toe.

The lift doors creak open on the second floor and Joe bounces out with Dave and Frank struggling along behind. '10.00?' Joe throws back his head and shouts with laughter. (He saw Jack Nicholson do it once and thought it looked quite manly.) No. No, no, no, no, no. I told Suzy last week to … well, here she is, let's ask her. Suzy poppet, I told you, didn't I, last week?'

'Yes, Joe. Hallo Frank, Dave. Um, er, told me what?' Suzy nervously straightens a stapler so that it lines up with the edge of the desk and waits as Joe grabs a buck with easy familiarity and passes it across to her.

Joe tuts and shakes a world weary head. 'Told you to call Dave and Frank and fix the meet for eleven o'clock today. Right?'

Already knowing the reply, Suzy feels she has nothing to lose. 'Wasn't it 10.00, Joe?' A convoy of paperclips join the stapler.

'I don't think so, lovey. I distinctly remember telling you 11.00 – same age as my son.'

(*See? There goes that lovely shiny buck, skidding to a halt next to the paperclips. And the fact is, Suzy has to give it another polish. Of course he told her 10.00 am. But who's going to argue with the Boss?*)

Joe sweeps past Suzy into his office, trailed by Frank and Dave. Every available surface is covered with old files, bursting with dog-eared paperwork. Joe pulls his coat off and hangs it on the floor, then plumps down behind his desk, while Frank and Dave have to find themselves a space.

Joe leans back in his chair and gestures benignly. 'That's right, boys, make yourselves at home.' Joe shouts out to Suzy, 'Couple of white withs for the lads …

(*note the use of patronising terminology under the guise of 'mateyness' – good for Subliminal Placement Retention, or 'SPR'*)

'… and I'll have a black without.' He pats his stomach – 'gotta watch the old waistline.'

Frank and Dave fuss with their presentation, propping concept boards up backwards so that Joe can't see them. While they are thus engaged, the phone rings. Joe ignores it. It continues to beg for attention. He still ignores it, then shouts for Suzy – there's no reply. The ringing grows more insistent. He shouts even louder. 'These girls, they're never here when you want them.' Finally Joe snatches the receiver to his face and barks the standard HCM opening down the line.

'I'm busy. Joe Manager. Whaddayerwant? Oh, hallo cocker – how's it going? Good, good. Nah, s'all right … just my agency boys – come to show me some pics for a promotion they've flung together. No, can't say that I do – dribble it past me again. Hmm, I think it rings a bell, and if it's the bell I think it is, then I'm sure – yes I know – I gave it back to you – I expect you've lost it! Ha, ha. Just kidding….'

Innocent and unsuspecting, Suzy bustles in with the coffees.

'Ah! Hold the front page, Bob. There you are Suzy! Talk to Bob would you, sweetheart? He thinks we've (*we've?*) still got his budget reports, but I told him, I'm sure I asked you to give them back, ooh, ages ago. Take it outside, there's a love. I really must press on with my meet.

Bob? Still there? Suzy's going to sort you out – you lucky man! Ha, ha, ha. And Suzy – try not to interrupt me for a while – no more calls, eh?' As Suzy walks out, with all the dignity she can muster, Joe shouts after her – 'unless it's the squash club.' 'Yes, Joe.'

Joe turns back to Frank and Dave. 'Sorry, lads, sorry – old Joe's a busy man. Right, now you've got my undivided attention

(*remember the BWP? No? Well, check the FMJ*)

– let's see what you got.'

Frank turns to the first page of a fat document. 'I think you're going to be pleased with what we've done, Joe, our creative boys have come up with a real winner. But before I present our creative recommendations, let's go back and re-examine the brief and objectives – Dave?'

Dave trawls a hand through freshly mown hair and takes up the story. 'Well, Joe, as you may remember, you had a bit of a problem with facings versus market share, through Buy-U-Rite. Our brief was to examine the ...'

Joe swings a scuffed pair of shoes down from the desk, where his heels have worn a smooth hollow caused by many years of 'laid back thinking' and bangs the flat of his hand on the desk top: 'yeah yeah yeah, I remember all that bizzo – cut the waffle and hit me with the pics'.

(*Here's a clue to the emotional age of the HCM – he's not interested in the bread and butter, he wants to cut straight to the jelly and trifle.*)

'Well, um, they won't mean much out of context, Joe,' replies Frank, adjusting a bordering-on-tasteful silk tie.

Joe counters by slumping back and casually loosening the knot of a polyester special. 'So, put them in a contextual framework, Frank,' he answers evenly.

(Does he want to hear the brief, or doesn't he? In other words, let's eat the jelly and trifle, but put it in a sandwich. The only discrepancy in this analogy is that when Joe's involved, it's usually everyone else who feels sick at the end of the party.)

Frank swallows and goes on. 'Oh, er, right. Will do. So, um, in order to ensure more facings, you have to create excitement in store, so the store managers really get behind the product and have a valid reason to display. Right?'

Joe looks Frank straight in the eye. 'If you say so.'

(A good phrase this. It warns the agency that a) either the HCM does not agree, and he's just about to tell them, or b) and this is more worrying – he simply isn't listening to them at all any more. 'If you say so' is just one of the key phrases that an HCM uses when he is preparing to pull the rug out from under a pair of Gucci loafers.

Other phrases of this ilk are: 'I hear what you're saying' and 'that's certainly what we've thought – up till now'. On the face of it, they sound like an agreement, but each one is really a 'no' in dark glasses.)

'Right.' Frank runs a nervous forefinger around the inside of his collar. 'Well, er, we thought of ways in which to achieve the level of excitement we were after, and our creative boys had a bit of a think tank, and . . .'

'And?'

'Well . . . oh, you tell him, Dave. It was you that sparked off the idea. I wouldn't want to steal your thunder.'

'That's very decent of you, Frank. So, Joe, we decided that basically yours is a fun brand – light, bubbly and a good all-rounder – just the sort of product that appeals to sporty, health conscious young adults ...'

Joe halfheartedly stifles a yawn.

(Never show interest in anything – it could put the price up.)

'Come on lads, get to the point.'

'... and so we thought we'd do a free draw promotion – no purchase required, as you know, Joe – but we'd offer an exercise bike which would feature in a huge product display, that would be terrifically impactful at point of sale. Then we could hire some pretty merchandising girls ...'

Joe has started slowly shaking his head. 'Sorry, fellas, no can do.'

Frank and Dave speak in unison: 'But why?'

'Because tempus fugit in the old marketing game and since I briefed you, I'm afraid events have overtaken both of us.'

(Events haven't done anything – but the HCM's in the driving seat and if he feels like doing a U-turn for no good reason, then he will.)

'They have?' Two pairs of eyebrows reach for the sky.

'They have. I could have sworn I told you – yes, I'm certain I did. The name of the game now, lads, is Ostrich.'

Dave, who had just taken a sip of coffee, chokes and has to be slapped on the back by Frank. 'Ostrich?' he squeaks.

'Ostrich', replies Joe. 'I'm moving Fizzmore into the nineties by sponsoring the London Ostrich Races – surely you've heard about it, it's all the talk round here you know – and just the sort of whacky, zany, off-the-wall idea that I want my product associated with.

'You know, Frank, we have to be adaptable in this great world of ours – can't stick our heads in the sand, you know – I want you to adapt this idea to promote my Ostrich Race.'

'But what about the tailormade for Buy-U-Rite?' wheezes Dave, imagining the impending confrontation with his creative department.

'Stuff the tailormade – we're talking Ostrich now, you know.'

(Always change your mind whenever possible – it keeps suppliers on their toes.)

'This is really going to put us on the map – or should I say lap? Race . . . lap . . . d'you get it? Ha, ha, ha – even when I'm under pressure, I've still got it!'

(Note the use of humour to diffuse a tricky situation.)

Frank takes a shiny gold Cross biro from his top pocket and unclasps his Filofax.

'Forgive me for being thorough, Joe, but let me just run myself by this one more time. You're asking us to forget the BUR tailormade, but adapt the creative work to promote an Ostrich Race – check?'

'Check.' Frank scribbles furiously in an already crowded 'action' section.

Dave has a sudden vision of a rather plump Creative Director kneeling across his throat. He rubs his neck subconsciously. 'Er, may I ask about the studio and executive hours that have already been spent on this project to date?'

(*Are they going to be paid for the work so far?*)

'They've not been wasted, Dave.' (*No*) 'After all, you're still going to use the basis of this material, so you can amortize the costs across into the new project.' Joe inspects his nails with an unusual degree of concentration.

'And what's the budget for this new promotion, Joe?' Frank's pen quivers eagerly above the relevant section.

'Who knows?' Joe leans forward to give his boys a final pep talk. 'Listen fellas, you know me – old Joe plays fair. You do your job – and I'll do mine. You come up with an Ostrich Race corker and I'll tell you whether we can afford it or not.'

(*This is a good one – you don't have to commit to anything and any idea they come up with is bound to be way over budget and they'll spend weeks trying to cut back, by which time they may have hit upon something that just about fits the bill. It's the 'I'll know if I like it once I see it' routine.*)

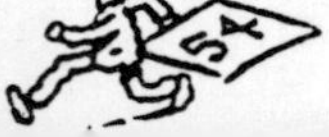

'And who's this promotion for?' Frank asks lamely.

'Londoners – I told you that just now. Try and stay with it, Frank.' (*Remember the SPR*[1].)

'Excuse me Joe, but what I meant was – what type of people, er, Londoners? Should we do an in-store promotion or a leaflet drop or a direct mail ...'

Joe waves his hand in the air. 'Yeah, whatever – you're the promotional whizz kids, or so you keep telling me – ha, ha, ha – so it's your ball game, logisticswise.'

(*He's given no thought at all to who his promotion is targeted at and why should he – after all, why buy an Ostrich and bark yourself?*)

'Er, right. And when do you want us to respond with promotional ideas?' Dave struggles manfully in the face of a waning attention span.

'ASAP, Dave'.

(*When he says it to them, it means he wants it yesterday, as opposed to when he applies it to himself, when it means 'after simply ages – possibly'.*)

'That old tempus, he just rushes right along and I've got Ostriches on hold. Pencil something in with Suzy on your way out, OK fellas? Don't mind if I carry on with some work while you see yourselves out, do you? I'm just so busy, busy, busy.'

Dave and Frank are dazed. Like men in a trance, they gather their possessions and stumble from the room.

(*And deep in his heart the HCM knows that it's all right to treat suppliers like that. After all, he's the client and if it wasn't for him, they'd never be able to afford their fancy offices and shiny fast cars ...*)

Footnote

[1] Subliminal Placement Retention

Meetings as a Principle

Not so much a principle, more of a pastime. The HCM likes meetings. Why? Because meetings involve people, and there's nothing the HCM likes more than saying 'this is a people business'. He doesn't like people very much, but he likes saying that he does.

And he likes spending quality time (buzz concept) with people – especially *his* people – geting input from people, hearing what people have to say and getting the best from people.

And he likes them to know that he respects them and their position – that he understands where they're coming from (buzz direction).

He also likes Meaningless Platitudes. And where better to spout MPs than in a meeting?

The proficient HCM has a number of Meaningless Platitudes at his disposal, such as 'let's stand in the lift with this one and see if it travels up' or 'I'm willing to put another penny in the peep show and see what exposes itself' or even 'OK men, bake those cookies – we'll see whether anyone dunks them'.

Meetings allow you to say things like that, because meetings are for groups, from whose safety it's far easier to carry off meaningless jargon.

The HCM loves meetings because he can have his say without having it rebound. Making a decision in a

PRINCIPLE OF COLLECTIVE IRRESPONSIBILITY

meeting means never having to say you're sorry. It's the Principle of Collective Irresponsibility. Or 'PCI'.

And while most of us may be annoyed to find our diaries full of meetings, because it means that we can't get any real work done, the HCM is delighted to find his diary full of meetings ... because it means he can't get any real work done.

It also allows him to use one of his own particular favourite phrases – 'Suzy had me in meets all day'. He's just such a busy man – too busy even to finish off his words properly. And such a busy man must be important. (By his meetings so shall ye judge him.)

A meeting is also a good battleground for an HCM, because it's full of cover. Nobody's going to stand up and say that you're a lazy incompetent bastard, because there's an unwritten rule that says you don't trash your colleagues in meetings – at least not if they're in the room at the time – because it makes you look bad for showing someone up in public. (This is not to be confused with honest to goodness bitching.)

If you're in a meeting with a number of people, do be careful not to pick the wrong man as an HCM study object, because meetings are where the little bit of HCM that lives in all of us likes to make itself known.

If your selected target says anything half way intelligent, you can be certain that he's not a true HCM. (Remember the 'Jekyll and Hyde' analogy and you should be all right.)

Anyone can sound like an HCM in a meeting

But broadly, the true HCM is the one who keeps repeating any, or all, of the following phrases . . .

'Well, I think George has raised a number of useful points there.'
(*I couldn't actually work out what any of them were.*)

'Not only has George raised a number of useful points there, but he clearly has the research to back them up.'
(*I couldn't understand what the hell everyone's talking about because George kept throwing bloody figures into everything.*)

'I think George has probably exhausted the possibilities along that line of thinking. Let's look instead . . .'
(*I haven't been listening and I'm bored, so let's move on to something else and I'll try again.*)

'I've got some figures here that illustrate what I'm trying to say. I think you'll be impressed.'
(*A junior colleague of mine has prepared some figures to back up an idea that another junior colleague came up with. I don't understand any of it, but I'm bright enough to realize that it's quite good and I'm going to take the credit for it.*)

It's this last point which is the most important, and as in all meetings, it's taken far too long to get there. A true HCM let loose in a meeting is more than just inattentive and a time waster – he's dangerous too.

For the HCM is a Credit Pirate and meetings are the high seas upon which he plunders ideas, murders projects in seconds that other people have been working on for months and always, always, somehow manages to move himself up in the estimation of any superior present.

And how does he do it?

With the 'IPTDIBSO Effect'. Loosely translated, it means:

> *'I Prefer to Deal in Broad Strategy Only'*

The HCM collects tiny grains of knowledge from a vast range of topics, enough so that he can talk broadly on a subject, knowing full well that he'll never have to take it further, because he'll always be able to delegate the actual work to some poor sucker within his control.

And nine times out of eight, the poor sucker wobbling blindfold at the end of the gangplank will be you – until you've mastered the tricks of the HCM trade and can cut the ties that bind you.

Another favourite HCM tactic is putting people on the spot in meetings

We call it the Principle of Deflecting Attention or the 'PDA'. And it's mainly called into play when someone's managed to back the HCM into a corner. Not that it happens very often.

But when it does happen, the HCM will suddenly and unexpectedly turn the spotlight on a victim, making him appear responsible for an omission on the HCM's part. It's awkward and potentially damaging to a career.

Aspiring HCMs should practice the PDA as follows:

select your victim,
put said victim on the spot,
and when they stumble and fail,
smile sympathetically and say 'never mind,
we'd better skip it then.
We're not blaming you.
these things happen – human error and all that.
Perhaps you could look into it and
report back at the next meeting.'

It works a treat. There is no retaliatory tactic. The victim can't come out of it looking anything other than awful. The more they protest, the worse they look – rather whiny and pathetic.

And did you notice how the HCM doesn't stab his victim in the back, but right in the front, in full view of everybody? And he even gets to twist the knife by saying '*we're* not blaming you'. Which means of course that *he* is – and everyone else is invited to do so too.

This is a good technique to employ when it looks like the spotlight is about to be turned on you. Even direct questions may be fielded by turning to a colleague for the answer, as if he was supposed to provide it. Their outraged denial is never that convincing if you maintain a mild mannered 'surprise' at such a response. Try and think of it a bit like ping pong – better to 'ping' that question back over the net, than 'pong' when the aura of a distinctly fishy answer surrounds you.

Where to sit in meetings

Always a tricky one this. It's best to be safely tucked up behind a desk – preferably your own – where no one can get at you.

However, sometimes you have to go out. And if the meeting is in someone else's office, then where you sit depends on whose office it is and who has called the meeting.

There are four categories:

1. Superiors
2. Clients
3. Inferiors and suppliers

Superiors

If the meeting is in your boss's office, then there are two preferred places to sit. Firstly, next to the boss. Now we don't actually mean behind his desk, with him, but as near as you can get without causing gossip. Why?

1. It lays down a sort of territorial guideline for the other attendees. (Somewhat akin to a lion spraying urine around the perimeters of his territory – not that we'd recommend this as a practical expedient.)

2. It makes you look important – as if you're his right hand man.

3. You can hand him coffee – a perfect opportunity for more 'I'm-a-warm-caring-human-being-so-I-must-be-good-at-my-job' acting. And it's just the ticket for avoiding eye contact – unless you're going to BWP[1], in which case eye contact is vital to provide that much needed, moist-eyed, sincerity.

4. If any tricky questions arise that you can't 'ping' away, then you are close enough to spill coffee in his lap or across the papers on his desk. This is always a good diversionary tactic, but use a minimalist approach for maximum credibility, say once or twice per meeting, unless you are prepared to pay someone else to do it for you too, on a pre-arranged signal. However, this can be complicated – and costly – to administer, and it leaves you open to blackmail – a reverse CIB[2].

Footnotes

[1] Black is White Principle

[2] Career Improving Blackmail

The alternative location is near the door. At the first sign of trouble, leap to your feet, clutching your stomach and make a bolt for the door. (Don't use it though, or you'll never get out.) This is always a good ploy, because by the time you come back in, the meeting should have moved on to another topic. If they're still on that 'sticky subject', double up again and crab walk out.

Use this last plan sparingly – repetition tends to dull performance (unless you're Placido Domingo) and leads to scepticism in the audience.

Now, the flaw in these plans is that HCMs are invariably late for meetings. That means that some other rotten toady may have pinched your seat. The brighter almost-HCM should have already spotted the solution … Of course – operate a BWP.

Enter the room in a rush and say to the toady who's in your preferred seat that there's an urgent phone call for them on their private line. If they ask who it is, tell them that the caller wouldn't leave a name, just that it was urgent *and* personal. If it's a man who's in your seat, say the caller was a woman, and vice versa. The toady will always leap up and leave the room to answer it and you can then take their place. Works every time.

Slow on the uptake trainee HCMs will need to know the following:

- it has to be a private line, because if it was on the communal switchboard, the call could be transferred to the office you are in;
- people only give the number of their private line to a select few – such as headhunters or girlfriends. Saying that the caller refused to give a name lends the bogus call an aura of mystery that makes it irresistible;

the toady has to take the call straight away as they can't say they'll call back, because they don't know who to call.

If you don't have any private lines in your offices, then say the call is on the toady's phone, it sounded urgent and you tried to get it transferred, but you couldn't and the caller is hanging on. That'll definitely get them moving ...

Meetings with clients

I'm OK—you're coming with me ...

Always take a colleague or inferior with you to client meetings. If you don't have such resources at your disposal (and if you don't, should you really be reading this book?) then flatter somebody into going, by saying that the client wants some advice that you're not qualified to give. It always works. Then once the meeting starts, you can just let the two of them get on with it.

The never to be broken rule is: don't go on your own.

If you can't help breaking rules (and no HCM can), then say you've lost your voice in the taxi and the lost property office was shut (but say it softly, or write it down).

And if that dodge fails, operate an SSP[1] – look in your diary, discover another meeting booked for whatever time it is at that moment, with someone in another company two levels more senior than your client (so he'll be impressed), sorrowfully blame Suzy (you can't get the staff, these days) and leg it out the door.

Footnote

[1] Secretary as Scapegoat Principle

The psychology of seating

Take whatever seat is offered (remembering not to sit behind the client's own desk), but try not to sit on a seat which is considerably lower than the one the client is going to use. This will put you at an immediate psychological disadvantage.

No, hang on. We all know that, don't we?

Even the client. So head straight for a seat markedly lower than his, sit down, look up at him and smile. He's bound to think there's some extraordinary psychological double bluff going on, so he'll try to work out why you sat there, if you've just put him at a disadvantage, and how he's supposed to respond.

This means that he'll have a hard time remembering all the tricky points that he was planning to score against you. And if he seems to be managing to score those points anyway, the Lower Seat Ploy, or 'LSP', allows you to play an extra diversionary tactic.

Just as he's firing on all cylinders about that third missed deadline, simply say . . .

> 'You know this is awfully clever, Neil. I've just twigged what's going on, you sly old bastard – my chair's a good nine inches lower than yours. You've been reading those psychology books, haven't you? And do you know, I bet if the sun was out, it would be shining right in my eyes, wouldn't it?'

Your client's consequent denial and sincere apology will defuse his previously angry tirade. He may be sitting higher – but you'll be in charge for the rest of the meeting.

One final point on seating – don't be lured into any of those snuggly, comfy looking sofas – you'll only fall asleep and snoring always draws attention to the snoree.

Meetings with colleagues

Standard HCM behaviour applies.

Sit where you like and deny everything – unless it's ownership of 'A Good Idea'.

Don't be shy about claiming ideas as your own that haven't been within fifty miles of your office – if you overheard it in the corridor, that's good enough for A Real HCM.

Meetings with inferiors or suppliers

The fast learning, up-and-coming HCM will ask 'why bother?'

That's good. You're certainly getting the hang of all this. But actually, there *is* a reason for having meetings with this sub-group. Sometimes they come up with A Good Idea and people with Good Ideas always want to talk about them and as you're A Manager, they'll want to talk to you. (Providing they haven't got wise to you yet.)

So go to their funny little meetings, act like A Leader – and soak up any ideas like a water biscuit soaks up saliva.

Two's too crowded– three's company

The only other point to remember about internal meetings is always to find out in advance exactly how many people are going. Technically, you can have a meeting with just two people, but never underestimate just how dangerous this can be, unless you've called the meeting yourself.

There's nowhere to hide and only you to answer any questions that may be raised. Meetings of just two people, when one of them is your boss, are particularly hazardous and may be likened to jumping from an airborne plane without the benefit of a parachute.

If you must have a meeting with just one other person, either:

a) don't, or

b) pretend you've got an ear infection and can't hear properly and insist your secretary sits in as well, to take notes. You can then blame her for anything untoward. (Remember the SSP?)

So, to summarise (and that won't happen often), meetings are – more or less – for stealing or presenting 'A Good Idea'. The thorny problem remains – how d'you recognise A Good Idea when you meet one?

Good Idea Detection

 ('GID')

You must develop the ability to detect A Good Idea from A Bad Idea. If you don't have a natural instinct for this, then sound out a colleague (never a boss) without saying whose idea it is.

If he holds his sides and screams with laughter, you can be fairly sure that the idea's a turkey – unless he's been reading this book and he's double bluffing you. (If it has red dangly bits on its chin and sports feathers, you can be certain.) Tell him whose dumb idea it was – you knew all along, but look what happened with Leonardo and the Hovercraft.

However, if your colleague keeps a straight face, nods a lot, starts finishing the ends of your sentences and begins to make notes – stop talking and leave. You're on to a winner, so go straight to the boss, in case the originator gets in before you.

Credit Control and the HCM

(or How to Protect a stolen Good Idea)

Having identified your 'Good Idea', you'll want to run with it. (Never walk, someone may jump you in the corridor.)

And with all those potential thieves about, you'll need **protection**.

If you work for an HCM, rule one is don't tell him your good ideas. Letting your superior know how intelligent you are may seem like a short cut to promotion, but if he's an HCM, that short cut is bound to be a cul-de-sac. Besides, if you promote A Good Idea yourself, it will reach a broader audience than if you leave it to your boss.

Persuade someone (money, violence or blackmail work best) to write an article in your name for the company magazine; work (we use the term loosely) in tandem with a colleague and present your ideas to his boss – even have your ideas printed on a t-shirt and wear it to the Christmas dinner dance. Anything, rather than hand them over lock, stock and Christmas bonus to someone who may out-chicken you.

If you 'persuade' someone to write a document for you, presenting your Good Idea, make sure they haven't introduced their own 'trademark' or 'autograph', so that it is clearly theirs without actually having their name on it.

If they have any particular hobbies, for example if they're known as an American football fanatic, make sure the whole forward projections section isn't a Superbowl play-off analogy. Unless you're into American football yourself, of course.

If you drive a Porsche and they take the bus, watch for careful comparisons between the efficiency of certain work practices and the efficiency of the local public transport system. People are jealous of success and they'll know you drive a racey motor and have never set foot on a bus in your life.

Remember, you told them to do the work in the first place because it's quicker and less stressful. But if they've inserted 'trademarks' all over the place and you have to remove them, not only does it make more work for you; it also means that you'll have to actually understand what the hell they're going on about, so you can put the information across in a different way. And that defeats the whole point of the exercise.

Now even if a genuine HCM was able to rework a document like that (which is highly unlikely), he wouldn't have time to do so, because an HCM never looks at any background material for a meeting until he's in the corridor outside the meeting room and the meeting's just about to start.

When you achieve full HCM status yourself, you'll be wise to all of this. So although you'll be delegating work like fury, you should resist the natural Chicken inclination to ignore all documents until the last moment.

That way you'll have time to take out any trademarks, so you'll still be able to claim the work as your own.

The HCM and Leadership

As an aspiring HCM, we've tried to give you a number of leads as to what to look for in your own HCM guru. But one of the other, rather strange, qualities that makes a successful HCM is that of apparent leadership. When coupled with the IPTDIBSO Effect[1] it is actually fairly devastating.

Footnote

[1] I Prefer To Deal in Broad Strategy Only.

The HCM's success stems from adopting a leadership position.

Actually he couldn't lead you into the sea off the end of a pier, but that's neither here nor there. He will always act like a leader and as Sir Larry would have told you – acting is everything.

Why?

Because Leadership is the egg in the soufflé of business success. And Leadership coupled with A Good Idea is the Roux Brothers' Dish of the Century. It's even more important than being able to use ridiculous cooking analogies like that one. (Although that's pretty important too.)

And though we can't all be paid like leaders, we can still act like them. So how do we do it?

Leadership is a quality that can't be attained by simply following a set of rules.

So here they are:

1 Leadership is all about people. Unfortunately.

2 People will only offer their full commitment to a leader in whom they have complete confidence. Unfortunately.

3 In the absence of full commitment, trust and confidence – fear is a good motivator. Fortunately.

4 (And this is the only one that matters.) Getting people to do what you want through fear alone is not the mark of a great leader. But frankly, my dear, who gives a damn?

(Another HCM trait is to plagiarise without getting the quote right.)

Imagine that leadership in business is like walking through a jungle.

The leader is the one who has to hack his way through the corporate undergrowth with a machette, clearing a path for the others to follow.

The HCM wouldn't dream of doing any such thing – he'd hand the machette to his secretary and stay in his office with a headache, so she'd be the one most likely to disturb poisonous client snakes, step into accounting quicksand or be picked-off by man-eating native suppliers. It's the SSP Revisited[1] – she must be twice as vigilant, expend twice as much energy and take twice as many risks as anyone else.

So always force other people to walk through jungles.

YOU JUST CONCENTRATE ON ACTING THE PART

Footnote

[1] Secretary as Scapegoat Principle

Techniques and Trappings

An A–Z Guide

Those of you who have been paying close attention, should by now have realised that it's the wrong thing to do. The Headless Chicken Manager is a Skimmer – dipping in and out of the Sea of Information, immersing himself just long enough to get his conversational feathers wet.

To put you in the right frame of mind for the start of your new career (hey man, tomorrow is the first day of the rest of your life . . .) we have prepared the ultimate Skimmer's Guide to Headless Chicken Management. A complete A–Z listing of the techniques and trappings essential for everyday HCM survival.

A is for Apoplexy A useful condition to detect, as a gauge for having gone just that smidge too far with a Chickenism. Signs to watch for are bright red cheeks, lack of coherent speech coupled with spluttering sounds, popping eyes. If you do spot this affliction in others – particularly superiors–stop whatever you were doing. If the condition looks particularly advanced, leave the room at great speed, saying you're going to look for water. (Don't bother with a divining stick at this stage.)

B is for Balls No, not that sort. Although having them helps (keep some in a tin, if you're a woman). We meant the 'juggling a number in the air' variety. Always have a number of Good Ideas on the go at once, you never know when you'll get caught short.

C is for Car Keep it racey, pacey and spacey. Remember, cars are a phallic symbol, so don't go driving a Reliant Robin if you're a Spitfire at heart. And alway pull away first at the lights, because it's an everyday metaphor for your working life (and your sexuality) and you never know who's watching – right?

C is also for Creative As in: I am creative; you are disorganised; he is about to lose his job.

C is also for Crisis And it's always someone else's. At one o'clock, restaurants are full of HCMs protesting that they really have to make this a quick lunch because 'things are going crazy back at the office/ranch/base/workstation/HQ – and they need my help'. (Needless to say, if it wasn't for the HCM, there wouldn't be a crisis.) At four o'clock in the afternoon, restaurants are still full of HCMs protesting that *this* really has to be the last drink because . . .

If you sense an impending crisis, find a 'working lunch' to go to and be sure to let your fellow diners know repeatedly what a sacrifice you're making in being with them, when your presence is so urgently required elsewhere.

D is for Denial I didn't. (The more emphatic, the better.)

E is for Employment HCMs like to stick with what they know – and who they know. They rarely change jobs unless the situation is unavoidable and when they do change, they always seem to land on their feet. It's one of the most irritating traits that denotes a true Headless Chicken Manager. Would-be HCMs please note that an Interviewer belongs in the same bracket as a Boss. Employ every HCM characteristic we've ever taught you – particularly Toadying and Acting the Part – to thoroughly convince The Interviewer that you're the only man for the job, so that he doesn't even remember that he's supposed to take up references.

E is also for Executive Toys Anything can be an executive toy, so long as it meets the following criteria:

- it's shiny
- it fits on a desk
- you've paid too much for it

F is for Friend Don't be tempted. They're time consuming, costly and they make you emotional. Unless it's your boss. (And then it's safe because it's only pretend.)

F is also for Fashion As in 'fab' or 'trendy' gear. The HCM isn't really interested in clothes – they can't earn you

more money, so what's the point? (Unless you're a fashion designer, of course.) The best piece of advice we can give you is: try not to draw attention to yourself. That means, don't dress in very expensive clothes and try not to wear spots and stripes at the same time. Come to think of it, don't wear them separately either. Imagine your clothes are so much executive Muzak – there in the background, but nobody takes much notice. Grey is a good HCM colour.

G is for Gearing Ratios ... gross margins, P&Ls, capex, overhead recovery, provisions, net contributions and all the other financial terms which the HCM doesn't understand, but uses whenever he wants to sound like a grown-up businessman.

The HCM wouldn't know a budget if you gave him one in a cage and the concept of capex goes right over his head. That's why he never authorises invoices or sends out purchase orders – after all, what's the accounts department there for?

And whatever the company accountant tells him about the dire state of the balance sheet, the HCM knows that accountants *always* have 'a little something hidden away to smooth out the bumps in the year end results'.

So don't you worry about overspending your allocation, agreeing a price that's less than the cost of production (give or take a BWP) or buying twenty years' stock because Suzy typed one too many noughts on an order you didn't bother to check. It's just a long term investment – and anyway, you can always sell it on to someone else. Can't you?

H is for Hope No one who has ever actually answered a question says 'I hope that answers your question'. Essentially the word 'hope' is a signpost pointing in the wrong direction.

Thus 'I hope that answers your question' means 'I hope you're too embarrassed to ask your question again, because then we'd all know that you didn't understand what I was talking about – and neither did I'. And 'I hope we can do business again really soon' means 'Thank goodness that's over'.

H is also for Hypochondriac – all the HCMs we've ever known. You've got an illness – they've had it twice. And not only have they had it, but they've got the pills to cure it in the top drawer of their desk – from an in-growing toe nail to brain surgery (you'll neeed a big desk drawer for the oxygen tent). They're also the only group of men to suffer from pre-menstrual tension and period pains.

I is for Me Exactly.

J is for Jargon There can never be enough. Use it liberally and invent new phrases as the situations arise. In the highly unlikely event that someone should ask you to explain yourself, sprinkle your explanation with yet more jargon. It doesn't matter if the jargon or the explanation make no sense – none of the best jargon ever does.

Superb for an on-going whitewash effect – particularly with clients. Mixed metaphors are always very satisfying too, as in 'you can take a horse to water but a pencil must be lead'.

K is for Kill Not really recommended as an HCM practice. In extreme cases of cock-up where even the most hardened HCM is starting to panic, remember that the Foreign

Legion offers a satisfactory alternative (although the food's not very good). Provided you leave the country before they confiscate your passport. (Secretaries are quite useful for organising travel arrangements.)

L is for Lunch Let's do it. HCMs like lunch – Power Eating we call it, or PE (a bit like physical education, but only the jaw moves) and a useful device for picking up A Good Idea when colleagues or bosses are under the influence of alcohol.

Key points to remember are:

- it's never your turn to pay
- stick to one bottle of wine or your GID[1] will be impaired
- only eat the pointy end of the asparagus
- don't eat the pointy end of the artichoke
- don't fillet the whitebait, you'll be there for hours
- blow out the flame on the Sambucca before you drink it
- cappuccino is the frothy one
- espressos don't come any bigger

M is for Mantra A Mantra is a sound or phrase that, repeated often enough, leaves the user in a state of peace and calm, transcending the cares and worries of the world around him. The HCM's Mantra is 'I'm in a meet, I'll get back to you'. If you say it enough times, it will solve all your work problems. However, you'll have to chant it again tomorrow. The English for Mantra is 'Meaningless Platitude'. Essential for surviving in today's business world.

N is for Networking Using other people's contacts as much as possible and keeping your own to yourself. (Why dilute a good resource?)

N is for Negativise Any word ending in 'ise' is a buzz word. Here are two other HCM favourites:

O is for Optimise

P is for Prioritise (Useful for making your sentences sound more important–and making them longer.)

Q is for Quasi Any word that you can attach to the beginning of another word, is also a buzzword. As is any word beginning with a prefix that ends in a vowel:

- quasi-scientific
- neo-monetarist
- socio-econometric
- psycho-demographic, and best of all
- quasi-psycho-socio-económic

The point of all 'ise' words and all prefixes is to further obscure the fact that you're not saying anything at all, thereby getting you out of tight corners.

'These sales figures are abominable, Joe.'

'I couldn't agree with you more, Sir, if we're staying within purely quasi-scientific economic measurements.'

'Er ... we are ... aren't we?'

'We can if you want. But let's not forget that last year was a year of prioritising goals within the neo-monetarist framework established by the present government. The time to optimise sales is next year.'

Footnote:

[1] Good Idea Detection

By next year, Joe will have done his statutory two years in Sales and will be in External Communications. Which is where he belongs.

Q is also for Questions The HCM asks 'Are there any questions?' when he doesn't want to answer any. It works like this: after the HCM has asked the question, he gives a quick look around the room, snaps shut a folder and says, 'right then, we'll move swiftly on.'

For the right effect, this sentence must be implied in the original question, so that anybody who dared actually ask a question, would be halting progress, wasting time, stopping the rest of the extremely efficient and clued-up team from getting the job done. It's all in the intonation.

Practice by asking 'how are you?' first as you'd ask a dear friend who'd been seriously ill, then as you'd ask a stranger with no insurance, who'd backed into your new car. Notice the difference?

Apply the latter intonation to 'are there any questions?'

R is for Realism In a meeting, the only acceptable way of saying 'get off my case, pick on someone else for a change' is to invoke Realism. Try 'this is all very well, but we have to be

realistic'; or, 'do try and live in the real world'; or, 'we went into this whole shooting match with very realistic ideas about what could be achieved'.

The implication is that your feet are firmly placed on the ground, while their head is in the clouds. They must then defend their position, which stops them attacking yours. Better still, their reply might veer into personal abuse which will put everyone else on your side.

S is for Strategy What can we say? The equivalent of a free period at school. The great advantage of Strategy is that you can leave the office early to go home, where the phones aren't driving you mad and you can *think* and develop some thoughts on Strategy in a more 'creative' environment. Especially during Wimbledon fortnight.

S is for Sport If God had wanted us to move that fast, he'd have put us on castors. Only indulge if you can win or if your boss has a particular favourite he can beat you at.

T Is for Tea To be suggested when someone you hate says 'let's do lunch.' It's an avoidance technique but you can make it sound the exact opposite. 'Look, I'm booked solid with lunches for the next three months, but make it a quick tea and I could squeeze it in next week'.

The great advantage of the Power Tea (or PT) is that it's short. As tea is so close to the end of the working day, it's hardly worth going back to the office, so people race through their tea in order to go home early. (PTs also make you sound like you're really busy, ergo important.)

U Is for Untrue (See BWP.) Key phrases to employ are:

- there's no hurry on this one
- don't worry, I'll field all the awkward questions
- you have my word this will go no further
- I thought of this myself
- really? I was in at 7.30 am
- I'm just slipping out to lunch – I'll be back at 2.00
- I don't know what happened, the line just went dead
- I left it on your desk
- that's funny, I sent it yesterday
- I was just about to ring you
- well that's what he told me
- it's not just me, nobody liked it
- I really went for it, but the others weren't sure
- if it was only up to me . . .
- I'll do what I can
- I'm not really the right man to ask on this one
- didn't you get my memo?
- the door to my office is always open
- I want people working for me who are so good, they make me frightened for my job

- there are no easy answers to this one
- any time you want help, just pick up the phone and call me
- I'd never ask anyone to do anything I wouldn't do myself

V is for Version Always stick to yours.

W is for WHAT?! Say it loud.

X is for Ex's The problem with expenses is that you become accustomed to a certain standard of living, which you cannot possibly maintain at the weekend. Unless of course, you patronise those restaurants that don't date their bills.

Remember the old adage that says if you want people to believe a lie, make it a big one? Doesn't apply to expenses. (Fraud is a separate issue.)

Y oh why oh why oh why . . . do I bother?

Z is for zzzzz If you must sleep in meetings, try not to snore.

Folifax Memory Jogger

The FMJ

BWP	Black is White Principle
CIB	Career Improving Blackmail
FMJ	Filofax Memory Jogger
GID	Good Idea Detection
HCM	Headless Chicken Manager
IPTDIBSO Effect	I Prefer To Deal in Broad Strategy Only
LSP	Lower Seat Ploy
MP	Meaningless Platitudes
OUCH	Obviously Useful Career Helper
PCI	Principle of Collective Irresponsibility
PDA	Principle of Deflecting Attention
PE	Power Eating
PT	Power Tea
SPR	Subliminal Placement Retention
SSP	Secretary as Scapegoat Principle
TT	Topic suitable for Toadying
WPC	Words Per Call

The Way Ahead

Well you're hardly going to find the way ahead back here, now are you? Frankly we're a bit disappointed that you've read this far at all. (Unless you've skipped straight to this page, in which case – well done, not that it will tell you very much.)

If you have dutifully read every last word, then you're still not quite ready for the rusty cut and flabby thrust that is the world of the Headless Chicken Manager.

Go back to the beginning and start again. And remember this crucial phrase . . .

> ***'The HCM deals in Broad Strategy Only'***

Conclusion

Oh you're not still here are you? You weren't really expecting us to come to any conclusion, were you?

Surely you've realised by now that the Headless Chicken Manager would never stick his neck out by drawing a conclusion. If he did, someone might chop his head off and, then he'd be ... ah ... now ... you probably think you can spot a flaw in our logic here, but in fact this is all going exactly as expected, given the parameters we'd set ourselves on Day One.

So if you'd just care to turn to page seven of the briefing document that we sent you last week ... WHAT?! You didn't get it? Suzy – why oh why oh why oh why do I bother? Oh this is ridiculous, we just can't carry on with this section until you've read it. We'll just have to put a red light on this and pick up the pieces later. Look, why don't I have mine call yours ...

No, not another word . . . we've gone home now.

Hawksmere – focused on helping you improve your performance

Hawksmere plc is one of the UK's foremost training organisations. We design and present more than 450 public seminars a year, in the UK and internationally, for professionals and executives in business, industry and the public sector, in addition to a comprehensive programme of specially tailored in-company courses. Every year, well over 15,000 people attend a Hawksmere programme. The companies which use our programmes and the number of courses we successfully repeat reflect our reputation for uncompromising quality.

Our policy is to continually re-examine and develop our programmes, updating and improving them. Our aim is to anticipate the shifting and often complex challenges facing everyone in business and the professions and to provide programmes of high quality, focused on producing practical results – helping you improve your performance.

Our objective for each delegate

At Hawksmere we have one major aim – that every delegate leaves each programme better equipped to put enhanced techniques and expertise to practical use. All our speakers are practitioners who are experts in their own field: as a result, the information and advice on offer at a Hawksmere programme is expert and tried and tested, practical yet up-to-the-minute.

Our programmes span all levels, from introductory skills to sophisticated techniques and the implications of complex legislation. Reflecting their different aims and objectives, they also vary in format from one day multi-speaker conferences to one and two day seminars, three day courses and week long residential workshops.

For a full catalogue of events, please call Hawksmere Customer Services on 0171 824 8257 or fax on 0171 730 4293.

Hawksmere In-Company Training

In addition to its public seminars Hawksmere works with client companies developing and delivering a wide range of tailored training in industries as diverse as retailing, pharmaceuticals, public relations, engineering and service industries such as banking and insurance – the list is long.

We specialise in all aspects of management development for middle and senior managers.

Hawksmere trainers are all professionals with sound practical experience. Our approach is participative, with extensive use of case studies and group work. The emphasis is on working with clients to define objectives, develop content and deliver in the appropriate way. This gives our clients total flexibility and control. In our experience, direct client involvement and support are prime contributors to the success of any programme.

Hawksmere In-Company tailored training provides:

- programmes producing real results
- expert speakers matched to your company profile
- flexibility of time and place
- maximum impact on productivity through training your staff at a pace to suit you.